MW00668734

Light through the Heart

The human heart can choose to be a receiver
Tuned to the wisdom of the cosmos,
Tuned to the frequencies of love,
Tuned to existence beyond the mind's comprehension.
This is the heart of evolution....

Terri

with much appreciation... and gratitude...

Jaimy Weiler

By Jaimy Weiler

Library of Congress Control Number: 2005901014
ISBN: 0-9766497-9-9

Published by ObeiLet Publishing
P.O. Box 7002
Huntington Woods, MI 48070-7002
ObeiLet@aol.com

Cover Photography from the collections of Judy Seldin
Symbol Design by Randal Secondino
Cover Graphics by Josh Visser
Printing by Thomson-Shore, Inc., Dexter, MI
Typeset in Papyrus Font
First printing, April 2005

Printed in the United States of America

Light through the Heart

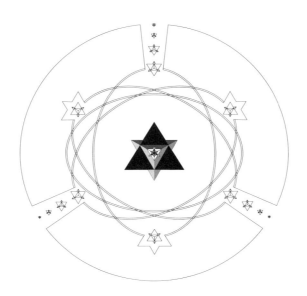

Open

I open to the source of wisdom.
I open to the source of words.

I offer my Self to be your graceful pencil, to glide across the page,
Attaching wings of freedom, breath and awareness
To small marks of graphite on paper.

Breathe through me Spirit, and let this pencil fly
To destinations unknown....

Table of Contents

Dear Ego   1

Ego   5

Unwavering Intent   7

Please, Say Yes   9

Stand   13

The Way Out   17

Life   21

Gently, Turn Away   23

I Call to You ... Wake Up   27

To Let Go of Everything ...   29

Evolution   31

Don't Waste Your Time   33

What is Enough?   35

Split-Level Life   37

A New Purpose   41

Awareness   45

Global Citizen   47

Wondering   51

Only Those Who are Asleep ...   53

An Act of Plenty   55

A Question of Money   57

To Have or Have Not ...   61

Location   65

Focus   67

Longing for Peace   69

The Source of War   71

New Insurance   75

Time   77

Balance   81

May We All Be Free....   85

Universal Self   87

Dear Ego

Dear Ego, my blessed friend Divine,

I take my Self to our beginning, so many lives ago.... The moment of our first incarnation, you and I. We came into being, together, to explore each other, to love each other, to come to understand this world and the shadow side of Spirit. We are God's creations, you and I. I have clung to you, learned with you, loved you. You have protected me, moved me, stopped me. We are travelers across all time. You are my companion, faithful and true, fulfilling your mission with me as you promised you would. I am so deeply grateful....

Remember the moment of our conception, of our coming into being? Oh so long ago our beautiful earth dance began. A spiral of cosmic DNA: light & dark, up & down, love & fear.... Me, on. You, off. Me, yes. You, no. My presence has defined you. And yours has defined me. We've been constant companions since that blazing moment of glory. The lives we've shared, that we've co-created, have been so magnificent, so richly textured. The struggles, the challenges, the tortures so real. The joys, the accomplishments, the braveries so exquisite....

And now, this traitorous moment has come. It has been coming all along. This moment when we are no longer equal, no longer partners together exploring this world. So sad, so deep, so unacceptable is this truth of our evolution. Who would have thought we would come to this?

How is it that I will carry on without you in charge? What will you do? I didn't know I would come to not need you. That I would become brave

enough to face incarnation without your fear and protection. Who knew that I would become God on earth? Forgive me, my friend.... I didn't know ... and yet we both have always known it would come down to this. Oh how I love you. You have served me so well, and I have been so faithful to your density. This sadness is to be respected. Together we must say good-bye to this eons-old way of being. We are evolving. I am now in charge. The tables are turned and I shall be your keeper. The past is done. Oh so well done. And you are relieved of duty. Rest in my arms. Rest in me, the magnificent earth-being you have helped God create me to be.

Ego

Love the ego through its death. Place strong and gentle arms around its despair and hold tight. Keep it from enacting its harm upon the world. Do not forsake it for even the smallest moment. Respect it, caress its snarling face with tender fingers. Bear its kicks and threats, knowing they are illusory and impotent to you, the true Self. Call upon every ounce of compassion for this ego, who will do everything conceivable to keep you from giving your entire heart to the light. See its desperation for what it is: the pain of pain and the loneliness of losing your allegiance. Do not mock or criticize this darkness. It suffers enough from the loss of power over you. It suffers enough in the contemplation of its own very real and impending death. Oh the depth of this sorrow ... may our hearts be strong enough to bear it.

Unwavering Intent

Help me to love. Help me to love a true love,
A deep love, a respectful love, a constant love....
Let my love be wise. Let my love be abundant.
May my love be perfect action, generously given,
Unannounced, impeccably placed, softly released.
Become me Spirit, as I become my Self.
So that I may be only perfect love.
So that I am only You touching the world.

Please, Say Yes

Oh, gentle hearts, what is it that you want? This noisy, cumbersome life often drowns out our deep, silent desires with its clamorous roar. What is it that you want? What do you long for? What do you deeply need for your happiness to bloom? Maybe it's time to know....

There is a tender spot inside, waiting to be touched. And touching this place in you will change the world. Where is this tenderness in you? This place that will tell you your deepest and highest desires? And give all the means to fulfill them. Will you find it? The world of the miraculous waits for us. Right there in that sweet and tender spot inside. The spot that is most often left ignored and unacknowledged in our daily life. Deemed unimportant in the hectic race against time and money. Perhaps we have even come to believe that it would be irresponsible to meet and fulfill these most essential needs and longings.

The quiet truth of the matter is reversed. It is altogether irresponsible to ignore and let wither these tender, deep desires. And so harmful to encourage others to do the same. Our societies and world crumble around us because we are dead. We are numb and offer so little real life to each other. Who can stay awake? Who can stay in touch with life, knowing that what one longs for with every fiber and cell of being will never come to be? Who can stay awake in the face of such cruelty? We are shut down to the true desires that would spring each one of us awake.

So I ask, what do you deeply desire? What do you long for and need? Touch that tender place that is brave enough to still be alive. Gently

touch your Self and awaken. Have the courage to say No to the world and Yes to your soul. End your personal cruelty. Stop ignoring the very essence of your life. It is so unnecessary to have a hollow life, lived in a cage made by superficial sets of cultural demands. Do what your heart calls you to do. Risk. Love. Spring yourself awake, and watch the world bloom around us all.

Stand

It's time to let go of struggle. Yes ... it's even time to let go of the struggle to let go of struggle. To just open up the hand and let go. See what happens.... Trust Self a little. Understanding the *why* of the clenched fist and holding on has had its day. Collectively, we've spent a good deal of effort on analysis and uncovering the why of our struggles and dissatisfactions. Collectively, we have an understanding of the effects of dysfunctional childhoods. At an experiential level, we know how fear limits us, how old and new anger delays our joy and pollutes our world culture. We even have awareness of how guilt keeps us connected to and stuck in the very past we may long to be free of. There is nothing left to do but let go. To take the risk of loving Self. Let go of the dark and move with confidence, trusting in one's own light no matter how faint it may seem. It's time to risk being wrong, looking the fool, being judged, being rejected, attacked or abandoned. It's time. We, collectively, have the strength to withstand these possible responses from the global ego. We, as individuals, also have this strength. It's time to focus on how many people are building light, holding light, being brave, letting go. The evidence is everywhere. Look for it. The small, quiet ways of love are all around us. Take a risk and be your Self. Time's a-wasting.

There comes a time when more understanding is counter-productive. We reach a place where we have to just let go of our fear and step out into the light and just stand there, without shrinking back, without explanation, justification or reason. To let go and stand there in the light of our light, and get used to being there. Without the protection of our mental life, without the defense of our fears. To stand in the light of

our own light without cover of darkness. This is freedom. This is what arises when one lets go of struggle. This is what is left for us to do. To stand strong in our light and let the attacking dark have no quarter, no space, no opening.

In letting go of our own darkness, the dark thrown toward us by this world can find no resonance, and so it falls impotent at our feet. Let go of the past ... all pasts. Let go of the explanations and understandings. Let go of regret, guilt, fear and anger. Open your fist and blow them ever-so-gently away. There just is nothing else left to do. And if a dark arrow should find resonance and lodge itself in you, pull it out and let it go. Pass your light over the wound it found in you and heal it. And move on. We've worked hard to create and get to this place of awareness, and now it's enough. It's time to understand that the dark does not protect us from the dark. Ego does not protect us from ego. It just keeps us in the darkness. Let go of it. Stand in your light. Be free. It's time.

The Way Out

There is such tightness and fear ... undercurrents of self-absorption leading us to treat each other badly, unconscionably ... justifying further tightness and fear. How can more protection of self-absorbed interests create safety? How can hoarding and consuming bring peace to a world where so many spend time only in the economic struggle to buy enough or to buy more? Those of us who have food, clothing and shelter and yet spend this day afraid for tomorrow, --with a closed fist around any amount of extra we possess-- create the very conditions we say we want to avoid.

The cycle is endless. Round and round and round. The only way out is out. To become neither a have nor a have-not. Leave the system behind. Become a steward. Become a trustee. Care for what is in your hands, be benefited by it. See yourself, in truth, as at most a temporary custodian, then pass it on. Use what you need respectfully. Don't hoard. Hoarding will make you afraid, make you act badly, cut you off from others. It will make your worst nightmares of vulnerability real possibilities. A heart that is bruised and dazed from being stuffed full of things, fear and self-protection can never be free. Can never afford to be fulfilled by real things. By things that are priceless and, therefore, free. These things are available to us all, haves and have-nots alike, if only we'd be brave enough to let go and choose them. Choose peace. Choose enough. Choose sharing ... both giving and receiving. Choose true kindness. Choose love. Even if only for five minutes a day at first. Build your power to choose. Escape the system of tightness and fear five minutes at a time. If we choose to do this, we will soon be living in a

different world. A free world. Even if we are the only ones who choose peace, who choose love. We will be living in a different world. We at last will be safe, safe in a way no material condition could ever provide. Safe from fear, safe from worry, safe from want. Safe to love and roll with life as it comes, as it goes.

Don't be a have or a have-not. Escape the system. The way out is out.

Life

Don't be fooled by death. Look deeply. Don't be fooled by aggression. Don't rise to the bait that disguises revenge as justice. Don't be fooled by death, by murder, by execution. See past this moment to the history of mankind. Death stops nothing. It never has. It doesn't end crime. We still have crime. It doesn't end war. We still have war. And death does not end the essential life. Murder does not end the soul, the Self. Life is far too strong to be stopped by merely killing a body. An act of fear can never destroy what is real. And death as an act of aggression certainly can't stop aggression. Can we yet see past this illusion called killing? It can't stop the true life within life, and it can't even stop itself. Death is so weak. Death cannot stop death. Aggression cannot stop aggression. These are only acts of powerlessness. And we collectively use these acts of weakness to justify our continued aggression, our righteous anger. We have much yet to see about the power of life, the power of love. We have a broader vision to cultivate so that we can truly see just exactly what is real beyond the illusions we place in this small, local moment. Don't be fooled by aggressive righteousness. Don't be fooled into believing that weakness is power. Don't be fooled by death.

Gently, Turn Away

Sometimes the only thing to do is turn away. To stop feeding insanity with your further attention. Insanity that wants to be insane will not be affected by your analysis, your admonishments or your proposed solutions. It will not heed or even address your cries of sadness, pain or despair. Insanity that desires to be insane is deaf to the calls of the common people looking to increase meaning, integrity and accountability. The best we can do sometimes is just turn away. Stop wasting energy and resources on that which will not look beyond its own self-importance, its own unending greed and self-deception. Without abandonment, we must find a way to turn away. To end the vast pillaging of our personal resources, our time, attention and money. Without abandoning that which we turn away from, we must find the courage to trust ourselves and turn toward sanity. To support and attend only to that which is simple, basic and fundamental to the global good. We now need to stop feeding evil by talking about it, by being appalled, aghast or shocked by what evil does.

What if we, without condemnation, turn away from the advertisers, the news media, the corporations and their products, the politicians and leaders who promote the common insanity? What if we stop fighting them and hating them? What if we stop giving them our time, money and attention? We can stop buying the stories, the dramas and deceptions, the addictive products and programs. We can stop complaining and criticizing. We can turn away. And turn toward our families, our friends, our selves and everyone else in our day-to-day world. And love them. With a respectful and mature love. And when we find we can't love so

well, we can use all the energy we were spending on the common insanity to teach ourselves how to love.

This darkness, this global insanity, when deprived of its diet of negative attention, opposition and aggression, starves and cannot grow. And when darkness is met by mature, unwavering loving-kindness, it, little by little, melts and dies. We must teach ourselves how to love. How to hold in deep reverence the worst this world has to offer. And not be seduced into joining it or opposing it. Just to love it. To offer it a strong, humble, compassionate heart. And turn toward and increase that which is sane in this oh so beautiful world.

I Call to You ... Wake Up

It doesn't matter, the color of your hair. It doesn't matter, the kind of house you have. It just doesn't matter, the degrees behind your name. It doesn't matter, the country you come from, the size of your bank account, your religion. It doesn't matter, your ancestral heritage, your addictions, your points of view. It just doesn't matter ... wake up ... wake up.... Our world is at war. We are cursing each other from our cars. We are becoming more and more medicated, more and more sick. Our meaningless, endless days are killing us. Wake up.... Our children are at risk, rage is rampant, the planet polluted, denial everywhere. Wake up.... Your opinions, your philosophy, your mental solutions don't help.... Wake up.... We are in actual danger from each other. Wake up.... We are killing each other, every day, every where. Wake up....

To Let Go of Everything
And Still be Here

We need to learn to take ourselves so seriously that we don't take ourselves seriously at all. It is critical for our evolution to let go of this preoccupation with what is personal, petty, local and small. Nothing can be resolved here. There is no abundance, no freshness, only conditional love to work with. These are not the building blocks of an inspired life or an inspired global community.

Einstein, oh our wondrous Einstein, said that a problem can't be solved at the level of awareness where the problem exists. You have to expand outward beyond the limits of the problem itself to see the solutions available. We are at this place.... We must expand our individual selves out beyond our ego needs, our nationalisms, our religions, our prejudices, fears and aggressions. Thousands of years of history demonstrate that politics, religious systems, economic growth and technology don't create the peace, safety and abundance we're longing for....

We, as individuals, one at a time, one after another after another, must expand past our small selves and our superficial personal concerns. It is our next evolutionary step, and we need to take it now. We have enough technology and enough rage to extinct ourselves. We are at a crossroads. Can you feel it?

Evolution

Evolution guides my soul
Carries me on a current of love.

Deeper than my awareness, Love directs my choices
And protects me from my worst intentions.

Evolution, a process I signed up for beyond my current consciousness,
Before I was born, in another state of being....

I feel my evolution in thought, emotion and bodily cells.
I see soul contracts fulfilled right before my very eyes.

To God, I am speechless, in awe and full.
To me, I am grateful. I chose to evolve.

God is faithful. And as an evolving soul, so am I.
Oh Bless Us All!

Don't Waste Your Time

Using your intelligence to love this world
Is a waste of time, a sham.... It is not up to the task.
It is too full of itself. It cannot master the skill.

Only the heart, broken open a million times,
Emptied of hope over and over, shattered ...
Can ever contain what it takes to love the whole of this world.

What is Enough?

What is enough? Enough of what? What, exactly, is it that you think you don't have enough of? Is it time? Is it money? Is it love? The right lifestyle? What about respect? How about power and influence? Safety? Security? Health? Beauty?

What, really, is it that you don't have enough of? Can you put your finger on it? Can you really name it? And then, as you experience not having enough, ask yourself, enough *for what?* What will happen when you have enough? How will you be able to tell that, finally and at long last, you have enough? How will you know?

So, what is enough? Enough is meeting the soul's desire for unconditional love.... For the unconditional security of knowing one belongs and matters to life. Enough is knowing that there is nothing one can do to be abandoned by life or made unimportant. Nothing. This is what enough is. Everything else is just playing Monopoly.... A little green house, a big red hotel or a giant pile of money can never be enough. Not even if you win.

Split-Level Life

Can there ever really be enough? What if there is something to the fear contained in this question? Perhaps the abundant life that fear says can't be real exists in a realm beyond this material life. This material life we're all so convinced is the only reality. What if fear itself can't comprehend the abundant life and is doomed forever to doubt it?

What if, in this realm fear calls "real life," there can never be enough? What if this is just the truth? Clothes wear out, cars break down, houses and buildings crumble, flowers die, objects of beauty fade away.... So, how can there ever be enough in this moment unless one was trying to get more in the previous moment?

Every day, somebody somewhere tries to take your glory, wear out your good reputation, steal your attention and capture your money with their products, services or opinions. Try to stockpile and someone will want to borrow it, tax it, insure it or steal it. They may already have what you have. But unfortunately, it's not enough. And it can't be. Because tomorrow always comes and more will be needed. What if we all acknowledged with great courage and conviction, "There will always be things I need. Now and forever...." And stopped being afraid of this truth.

As long as we have a material self, we will need material things. And the things we need will evolve and change as we evolve and change. Now and forever. Until we are no longer part of this material world. This truth is a constant trigger of our fear. We can never have everything. There will always be things we don't have. Other people own these things. Or, if

they still belong to nature, we fight each other to make them our own. And as soon as someone else has something, fear wants and needs one too. So, since we can't ever actually own everything and everyone on the planet, including the earth herself, fear will never have enough. The simplest truth is that, for fear, nothing is enough. Nothing is ever enough.

Nothing is enough. Nothing is enough. It's a split-level truth. In the material realm of fear and ego, nothing will ever be enough. More, more and more is always needed. *Nothing* is enough!

However, in the reality of love found deep within and surrounding the realm of everyday thought and fear, nothing *is enough*. Nothing *is* enough. Having nothing is enough! No *thing* is "it." Only love is "it." No thing fills us up. No thing makes us safe. No thing proves our value. No thing satisfies our hunger. And we stop pretending things ever could. In the realm of love, the way to experience enough is to *be* enough. Right now, in this moment, as "things" currently are. Be safety. Be valuable. *Be enough....* Experience the truth of enough through the vibrations of love.

The reality of love changes everything. In love, enough is the constant, the steady state of existence. Satisfy your hunger. Become love. Be enough. Because, in truth, you can never *have* enough.

A New Purpose

Do you really want to focus so much of your wondrous life working to pay for things that, by definition, can never end your fear? That can never give you the experience of enough? Do you really, truly want to spend your precious existence working to buy, replace, clean and repair things, feelings and loyalties? Things, feelings and loyalties that will never let you rest? Never help you *be* enough? By all means, we are free to do so. And many of us do. But by no means is it required. No matter what our families, governments, religions, advertisements or economic theories tell us. It is not required that we live unconscious lives, responding to the cues and controls of external authorities who are numb and oblivious to the heart's calls for love, life and deep community....

Who owns you? Do you realize how much of your daily awareness and action "society" controls? Who is it that chooses and runs your reality? Wake up. Lift your life, your consciousness and your heart up and out of the realm of fear and common sense. Vibrate your awareness out past this fear-filled mental arena where everything is dangerous and nothing is enough.

Ok ... let's say we choose to focus our lives on something other than the realm of "not enough." Let's say we choose to lift our life's vibration into the world of love, the world of enough. We still need to eat, be clothed and be housed. We still need to have things and to care for them. Of course we do. But what if we spent only 20 percent of our day in activities related to acquiring things? And then viewed this time spent making money as an act of creativity in exchange for money? Joyfully,

creatively, we would produce and manufacture the things needed locally and globally for our daily lives. Without excess. Without lack. Ahh....

What if we spent the remaining 80 percent of each day being satisfied with what we have and enjoying what is all around us? What if we spent our time growing, sleeping, nourishing our bodies and hearts, loving self and others and caring for the earth beneath our feet? If 80 percent of our lives were spent in these ways, we'd need so much less money, much less health care and entirely fewer things. We'd be deeply satisfied and have leftovers to share. We could live our lives now, today and every day. Retirement would become obsolete. What would there be to retire from but a life filled with love and creativity? We'd actually just live, really live, till we die. What an idea! An idea whose time has come.... I vote yes. What about you?

Awareness

So, you really believe that celadon mug, with the oriental character for peace so beautifully crafted into its side, will actually bring you peace? Of course you do. We're supposed to. At least while it has our attention in the shop and as it consumes our money at the checkout counter. But the illusion lifts after about a week in the kitchen cupboard, when you've not actually used it yet and drunk up all that beautiful peace it offered in the store. Or you've used it, but not actually gotten more peaceful or even looked deeply at it since you brought it home. Here's a bottom line on this: It's sitting down and drinking a cup of tea with your Self that offers peace. It's not the mug, not the tea, nor the table, not the space. And it's not even the weather outdoors. It's being with our Selves. And that never costs even a penny and often requires less than five minutes.

In truth, there is peace and fulfillment in that mug. Especially since you can just feel how beautifully it was created. The energy you feel was put there by those who conceived and created the mug. They share it with you. But it can never be yours. You can only borrow it, be inspired by it. But you can never own the peace, even if you own the mug. Another bottom line here: We have to create our own peace and fulfillment. The emphasis is on creation. Creation itself offers peace, offers satisfaction. The act of powerfully creating time for tea with one's Self.... So, stop. Stop putting your deeply valuable time, money and attention into buying stuff. Excess stuff. Stuff full of marketing illusions and seductive promises. And if it's not yet time to stop, become more aware of what you're actually buying. A cup or the hope of peace?

Global Citizen

Think twice before you buy something. The item you are about to buy has a history. Maybe a long history. Maybe a short history. Either way, it has a story of how it came into being. If you wonder about the journey this object you're about to make your own has taken, you can more deeply appreciate the world and your own place in it. Ask questions as you wonder, as you think twice. What are the raw materials used to make this item? What part of our earth did they come from? Were they harvested, fished or mined? Who are the people who collected those materials? Do you think they enjoyed their part in creating this wonderful item? Who designed, manufactured and shipped it? How far has it traveled? Did it move here by plane, by train or by ship? Was it refrigerated? Did it come in a box or a bag? Maybe somebody owned it before you. So many steps this item took on its journey to you.... It is a beautiful thing to consider an item's history, to touch in with a world of events outside our normal daily routines. It is a chance to see how supported we are by the efforts of other people across the globe and by the bounty of this earth.

Thinking twice before buying gives us pause to contemplate the nature of our actions and to consider our impact as a citizen of earth. Buying is like voting. We cast our vote for this type of manufacturing and this kind of work environment. We vote on other people's wages. We vote for this type of farming, this type of pesticide. Or we vote for no pesticides at all. We vote on how people and the land should be treated. Every time we buy something, we cast our vote for many, many things in this

moment-to-moment continuous global election. Considering an item's journey helps us to be wise voters. After all, every vote counts in our global economic community.

Buying is also signing up to be a steward or caretaker. Do we use the item we have purchased well? Do we care for it and make the best use of it we can? Do we refrain from buying what is not needed so that it can serve where it is needed? Do we use what we buy to serve and increase the health, life, light and true happiness of ourselves and the world? Buying something, and the actions that follow, speak volumes about what we value and who we are. Think twice, vote your heart and love the world.

Wondering

How many times have you been out driving in the spring and seen the beautiful flowers, plants and trees? The wonderful landscaping, the new varieties of the season in your neighbors' yards? And then in a flash, you begin to assess your own garden, wondering when, where and how you can get some of those flowers you just saw. How much will they cost? Do you have time to plant them this week if you go and get them? Stop.... The offering of beauty all around you is going to waste. You could be experiencing all these plants and flowers in their glory right now. For free. Without making time to fit them in. Right here. Right now.

This is the real abundance of life. It's everywhere, all the time. But the path of acquisition consumes our minds, consumes our lives. We think we can't or don't enjoy something unless we own it. And even when we do own the plants, flowers and trees, they don't quite seem to give the hoped-for beauty but become another "to do" on a list already bursting at the seams. We don't need to own something to experience its gifts. What is this ownership thing anyway? It's something worth wondering about.

Only Those Who are Asleep Will Buy Something That's Free

Happiness can't be bought. It's free. And as soon as you try and buy it, by definition, it's not happiness you get. Oh, you may receive an experience or sensation that is pleasant or even terrific. But like always, the pleasure fades, and the search for more begins again. You can't buy happiness because it's free. It's everywhere, all the time. The belief that you can buy something to make you truly happy is the actual source of unhappiness. Let go of the belief that anyone or anything but your own true Self can make you happy, and happiness becomes visible all around you. At no charge. And the supply is endless. But you have to have the courage to weed out the thoughts that say happiness comes in this package, this promotion, this person. You have to be relentless in un-brainwashing your self. Clean your mind. Clear your vision. Lift the heavy veil of consumption that has settled over your eyes. Then you will see that happiness is free. That happiness is a state of being, not a state of having.

An Act of Plenty

If you are feeling parched and lonely, practice looking deeply. Pick anything and look at it with your heart. Give yourself the luxury of looking for more than a brief moment. Make your looking seeing. Make your looking an act of intimacy with life. See the object you've chosen, be it a flower, the face of a friend or a bit of trash. See it with your heart wide open. See its life, its history. When did it come into being? What did it come from? Why these colors, textures and shapes? How did nature create this? How did humans create that? See how Spirit is in every act, every moment of creation. Every single act. Appreciate the journey of your chosen object, your intimate friend in this moment of seeing. Allowing wisdom and awe to arise in you will water your soul on a dry and dreary day. Seeing deeply is an act of plenty that can banish even the fiercest illusions of lack.

A Question of Money

This is an offering of freedom. A chance to go exploring outside the box. To see if we can spot something new, something fresh, something to bring relief to a broken-down system. A chance to question this mess we've made around money, with question after question leading God knows where. Ready? Let's go....

What if how we deal with money is a mirror for how we deal with the divine essence in our lives?... What if our individual relationship with money is a physical acting out of our internal relationship with Spirit? What if our response to money is evidence of the true nature of our response to our own divine Self? What if it is as simple as that? What if money is just a road map showing us our own personal way back to our divinity? What if money has no meaning except that which we, as individuals, choose to give it? Not a new concept, to be sure. But what if it's actually true and not just a concept?

How do you explain your monetary life to yourself within this context? If money and your divinity are one and the same, what are you doing? What does it mean to you if you have a big income and very little freedom? How does that relate to your essence? Are you selling your soul to get money? How does that fit with your experience of what you think God requires of you? What does making only a little money mean to you? What does it mean to you to know that you most certainly can create beautiful, wholesome wealth and yet you don't or won't?

What does it mean to you if you have a lot of debt? Is God/money coming in the future but not today? Or is your debt in the form of divine investment and trust in Self and the Selves of others? How does

having a great stockpile of money and still being afraid it's not enough relate to your experience of the spiritual life? How does it feel to have more than enough money and yet not allow yourself to touch it out of fear for the future?

What does spending mindlessly on temporary satisfactions say about one's relationship to the divine? What does the choice to buy insurance tell you? What do you feel about people who hold onto their money until their death? How do you deal with people who want your money? Or people who don't? How does not being able to move in life without counting and recording every penny affect your Spirit? Or, how does not putting and keeping your financial life in order impact the quality of your divine life?

Do you resent money or those who have a lot of it? Are you rigid or tight or loose or scared? Do you hide money from yourself or put it into vehicles with "heavy penalties for early withdrawal" so that you won't spend it? Or do you spend it so that you can continue to feel like you don't have enough? And if you put off having a lot of money now and only hope for more in your future, are you putting off your true divine empowerment?

What do you really, actually do around money? What do you feel? Do you feel? Do you know? What power do you think you get from money, and yet with all the money you've had pass through your life, you still don't feel powerful enough?

There are so many beautiful questions to ask ourselves about our money life. Questions whose quiet, deep and true answers lead us inevitably home to our own divine Self. The Self that always creates what is needed in every moment and is never burdened with getting or holding onto that which is not of true value to life.

To Have or Have Not ...
That is the Illusion

Ok. Let's travel into taboo territory.... Let's look beyond common convention with our heart's wide open. Let's dare to challenge our global mind-set, to risk being called cold-hearted or crazy. Let's break free of this illusion....

Money in today's world is so heavy. So very dense and distorted. Many, many souls are weighed down and imprisoned in illusion by the heaviness of their abundance. While many, many other souls are blind, groping in the dark, needing more under the heavy cloak of poverty. Both states are illusions created by the vast and rampant fear running loose on our planet. True abundance is never heavy, never a prison. And poverty isn't real. Let these words resound and echo within you. True abundance is never heavy, never a prison. And poverty is not real....

The illusion of abundance:
The weight and imprisonment of abundance are only thought-created feelings. Words of greed and potential loss strung together by a fearful global mind, turned into gut-wrenching, soul-numbing feelings that cause many wealthy people the world over to buy insurance, stockpile money and hoard goods. To live work and family lives that are intolerable and to push all the poor have-nots away with great fear, anger and political might. Wealthy people are so susceptible to this heavy emotional poison.... This heavy emotional poison blows like a hot and scorching

wind across our planet, destroying everything in the path of its greed and consumption. This is not true abundance.

The illusion of poverty:

The blinding haze of poverty is also a thought-created feeling. Created by the same fear-struck communal mind stringing thoughts of lack, hopelessness and apathy together to create feelings that cause the impoverished of this world to shut down their vision. To become numb to possibility, to lose sight of deep Self-respect. These mind-words of fear cause blindness. The impoverished eye cannot see the number of leaves on a tree, the number of grains of sand underfoot. The true abundant nature of reality stands before the impoverished eye and is invisible. Money does grow on trees, but you must have clear vision to harvest this truth. The blindness of poverty is a heavy emotional poison, too. And this poison vibrates our atmosphere like visual white noise, hiding the truth of our natural abundance in a snowstorm of illusion. Poverty is not real. Such a taboo thought....

Oddly enough, the imprisoned haves and the blinded have-nots are equal. We are all in the same struggle – we merely represent six billion different positions on the spectrum of have/have-not in a world of illusion. Rich is not safer than poor. Poor is not more spiritual than rich. Neither state has anything to do with true happiness. Both lack meaningful power in an awakening world. Both live in a state of war with the world, either as victor or as victim. Both can be equally void of peace, void of the blessed rest deep truth brings.

Wake up. Wake up. Let go of the stockpiles. Open your eyes wide to the opportunity and abundance in every moment. When you need a mango, pick one. Let go of illusion, the hot wind, the visual white noise. Let go and notice that you live in the Garden of Eden. Right here. Right now.

Location

Sitting in fear, everything's fearful, everything's dangerous.
Sitting in fear makes so much fear.

Sitting in Self, everything's selfless....
Every word a blessing.
Every thought service.
Every action needed.
Every thing enough.

No end to pleasure....

Focus

There are plenty of distractions in the world. Both the inner and outer world. Plenty of opportunities to be called away, to do things, to think things, to feel things. Distractions are endless. Their numbers are limitless. Best learn to focus, to be powerful in the face of distraction.

Freedom comes in facing distractions and then turning away. Over and over and over again. Till a moment comes when distractions rage all about and one responds only from a place of fluid, natural peace. Suffering no distractions at all.... Oh! What a delightful moment! Such Freedom! Imagine stringing moment after wondrous moment together, transforming one's very own life into a magnificent and unending walk of awareness, focused only on love.

Longing for Peace

Here I am, floating on this pond.

Paddling my feet gently, going nowhere in particular. Happy.

Looking around, absorbing the sunlight. Being a creature of Eden.

Why is it then that I long for a little chaos, some rough water to navigate
or rain to endure?

Oddly enough, remaining at peace takes practice.

And so, I practice.

Soon enough, the rough water I wished for comes with rain to endure....
And then, I long for a still pond, a little sunshine.

Peace takes practice. And so, I practice.

I practice in sunshine. I practice in rain. In storms and on quiet days.
When I am hungry, when I am full, I practice.

Until I have become peace,

And longing makes no sense.

The Source of War

It is true that peace can be confused with boredom. It seems that when too much peace breaks out, the small self becomes unsettled and looks about for something to occupy its attention. Anything to alleviate the anxiety that arises as peace swells forth.

The small, local self will turn to anything to escape peace, using fear and aggression (often falsely disguised as love ...) against self and others to stir the mental pot. There will always be something or someone to fix or care for, something to clean, something to worry about, big issues to solve, enemies to subdue, etc. This small and incessantly active self will forever choose to distract us from the peace all around us in every moment if we do not take our own personal steps to stop our selves.

The anxiety which initially arises in the midst of peace can and must be healed. It is a requirement of our spiritual maturation, our spiritual evolution. In order to become the true, spiritual human adults we are offered the opportunity to become, we must leave our adolescent ways behind and teach ourselves to sit still internally, to be at peace. We must bring ourselves to understand that action taken out of boredom or anxiety leads only to war, whether large and global or small and personal. It leads only to the inappropriate use of our personal and global resources. Action taken out of boredom or anxiety will always be aggressive. Will always harm self, other, or our land. As spiritual adults, we must grow this part of ourselves up. We must surrender our need for stimulation, busy-ness and immediate gratification. We must teach ourselves to handle peace. To see that it is everywhere until we disrupt it. We must teach ourselves to be in it. To sustain it. To cultivate

peace in the presence of our own agitation, anxiety and boredom. To completely understand that the boredom-alleviating quest for more and better, the righteous need to problem-solve and our unending productivity will never bring peace. Never. Since these don't bring us peace today, and haven't ever in the history of humankind, how will they in the future?

Peace is always present. It is the steady state of existence, the backdrop of life. It is the field of awareness where creativity and love dance and sing together for all eternity. Coming and going. Becoming and un-becoming. Peace is always present.

Our choice to remain fearful, aggressive and anxious, calling peace boredom, only obscures peace from our view. But it is always there. And in a heartbeat, we can return to it. We can teach ourselves to remain in peace and to ride out the boredom and anxiety until they subside. We must. We just must. We can refuse to act until our vision clears and the gentle wisdom of Spirit takes the place of our boredom and anxiety.

We must mature ourselves now and know beyond knowing that fear, anxiety and boredom can only create war. The war that for so long has captured our precious attention, leaving no room for the awareness of peace.

New Insurance

An expanded heart with compassionate awareness is the truest form of insurance available. Every situation, no matter how dire seeming, has a next step. The step that leads to greater love, peace and the true meeting of needs. It takes a commitment to awareness to see this next step. Not payment on an insurance policy. Life is truly all flow and nothing but flow, courageous step after courageous step. Open up, open ever more in trust to the love and care that is always ready in the background of the heart to help us carry on.

Time

Time is wildly abundant, as is everything on this planet. That is to say there is a lot of it everywhere, all the time. Nothing but time. Time after time. Time and time again. It's endless. And just like with money, it all depends on how you choose to spend it. It's yours. Every second. Yes, every second, now and forever. You set the price on every second you experience. Ok, so you already know this. At least with your intellect. But do you really give your heart the freedom to act as if it's true? Can your body get a word in edgewise when your mind spends endless amounts of time doing things that hurt it and your heart, or at best ignore them? No, I really mean it.... Do you have the courage to wake yourself up and know that you are responsible for the quality and content of every single second of your personally allocated moments of life?

How many seconds of this current hour are you willing to spend feeling frustrated or unhappy? 300 seconds? That's five minutes. Are you sure you want to trade five of your very own minutes for frustration or unhappiness? Maybe you'd rather trade them for a stressful job with inadequate pay. Or maybe some love affair with junk food, or a numbing relationship with your television. Many of us choose to spend our minutes complaining about the government, our enemies, the weather, our families, co-workers or friends. Or better yet, our selves. This is always a tempting one. It seems a lot of us buy shame and personal recrimination with our precious time. A truly popular item. Another big seller is personal aggrandizement and being right. Many, many seconds,

too many to count, are spent on this globally each day. This is why we continue to create war together.

It takes courage and the state of being fed up with accepting such poor quality to begin to shift your time budget from buying harmful worthlessness to buying what your true, deep heart desires. What your true, deep heart has desired since the day you were born.... As children, we may not have been in charge of our time or what we received in exchange for it. But as adults, we are. We are totally in charge. Yes, *totally.* Truly. You say, "I have kids; I can't leave my job." Yes, yes you can. You certainly can. I am not even remotely saying you should. How could I? How could anyone say that but you? What I am saying is that it is your choice and your choice alone. Of course, we consult with others regarding how we spend our time. But just remember who ultimately owns your time.... You. Steward it well. Use it for the true benefit of the planet, your loved ones, your family, your self, and even for the true benefit of those you think you hate. You'll feel better.

Empowerment, freedom, wealth and the experience of abundant time come when you deeply own the fact that every second of your life is under your direction. Whether you direct yourself on purpose or follow internal and external cues unconsciously, it's still your choice. Every second that passes, every minute of every hour of every day is yours. You are rich. Rich! For a moment well spent is more beautiful and fulfilling than an entire lifetime spent on self-betrayal, false goodness and greed. You have a million billion moments. Spend them well.

Balance

Amazingly enough, procrastination is a form of soul abuse. As an effective yet subtle method of Self-deprivation, it causes the soul to starve and the material life to stagnate and become unmanageable.

To put off soul-enriching, soul-expressing activities creates one's life to be a hopeless, seemingly endless desert. We long for peace, relaxation, freedom and joy but put off the very things which will carry us immediately to this oasis of fulfillment. "Maybe tomorrow I'll take that walk." "You know, this fall I'll start guitar lessons, when things calm down." "After the house is picked up, I'll put on some music and begin to dream...." "When the kids are in college, I'll write that book I've been longing to write." This is soul abuse. It is Self-deprivation. It is torture. No, I do not exaggerate. Hear me. This is a personal form of terrorism, of aggression. The soul, by nature, longs to experience the power of creation while in human form. It longs to dance and intertwine with the Divine in the act of expressing its joy, wisdom and beauty. Recognize the truth of procrastination. Of putting aside or putting off the beautiful urges of your creative force. Become conscious that you are starving yourself, denying yourself a cool drink of refreshing water in this parched and hungry world.

On the other hand, to put off your material-world activities and responsibilities is also soul torture. The soul longs to be current, to be up-to-date and in integrity, to rest in a job well done. To procrastinate here creates only fear and uncertainty. Balance your checkbook. Do the laundry. Fix the car before the damage expands. Become aware of the fear, anger and heaviness that putting these things off creates in

you. Keep current with your worldly duties as an act of mercy to yourself. Being tired while doing what needs to be done is difficult. But it is noble and soul-respecting. *Being tired and not doing what needs to be done is not restful.* It only expands the burden you carry and increases your tiredness. Pay your bills and rest while doing it. Teach yourself the truth about procrastination. Stop the torture. Don't believe yourself to be self-caring when you say I'll do it tomorrow. Look deeply. Resting while doing leads to being. Being is a way of life. Bring all those things you need to do into the flow of Spirit. Get up and begin, rest and flow, doing what needs to be done. Become one with being in the activity. Don't resist. Suddenly things are done, up-to-date, nothing to put off. No great weight of the un-done to carry.

Move, flow, create, attend to.... Restful activity that cares deeply for the quality of both your material *and* creative life. Attend to your worldly duties. Every day. Express your soul's powers of creation. Every day. Stop the abuse. Now.... Terrorism is out of control on our planet. Out of control.... Do your part. Stop terrorizing yourself. Stop killing your life force. Stop holding yourself hostage. Do your part for peace ... today.

May we all be free....

May we each become our own true Universal Self....

Universal Self

Oh, my Universal Self, I travel my bridge to You.

I journey back and forth, a confused pedestrian

Participating in an evolution I barely comprehend.

Oh, my Universal Soul, so self-evident, so complete....

When I cross my bridge to you and become our true vibration,

My endless questions lose their appeal. My fears become boring,

And I have no interest in keeping them bound so tightly to my existence.

Oh, my All That Is, bless my coming and going.

Keep me patient as I travel toward and away. Hold with me my heart,

Till I come to rest in You, my Universal Self, My Universal Soul.

Never to leave again. Then, as One, we will traverse this bridge together,

Bringing in light, light and more light to this magnificent and evolving world.